JANE DUNCAN ROGERS

7 Steps to Thinking Rich

*Essential Inner Tools for Abundance, Prosperity and
Wealth in Your Spiritual Business*

Contents

Preface

Do you want to support your business or project, express it's heart and soul, and express yours too? Put in place these 7 Steps and welcome in enjoyment, fulfillment and delight, for both you, your colleagues and your customers!

In 2008, I had been through the process of making a lot of money from the sale of a previous business, investing most of it, and then losing it all in the credit crunch at that time. There's a whole story there that gets covered in other books, but suffice to say, I had to learn to put each of these steps consistently into practice, and I still do. This book is the updated edition, incorporating lessons I have learnt since then.

Rich thinking is an attitude, a commitment and a way of life. Read on to be inspired to become a happy and successful Rich Thinker!

When the word 'rich' is mentioned, people tend to think only of money, and yet true riches, while it includes financial abundance, is about far more than just money. There are many people in the world, with small or large businesses, who have plenty of money and yet cannot be regarded as rich because they are unhappy, lonely, lacking in purpose, love or any of the myriad things that go to make up a truly rich life. If that's the case, then what is the difference between someone in the same physical situation as someone else, but one of them feels awful, while the other feels fine? It boils down to how you think, and how you are responding to the situation you find yourself in. That leads into how you feel, and of course that affects your actions.

So if you are gnashing your teeth because you're aware your attitudes to money are interfering with your business success; or nothing you're trying is going right; or you're frustrated at the amount of time it's taking to achieve your goals, know that all of these things are best changed from a starting point of knowing the place of true wealth in your life.

That place of true wealth is the source of life – that indescribable essence that is all around us, within us, and also within all the great spiritual traditions; that is a source of huge compassion, love and support when times are hard. This essence, whether you call it Divine Energy, God, Allah, the Universe, Light, whatever – is the guiding principle in my life and business and the sacred bowl out of which rich thinking comes.

Having said that, this book focuses more on money than on other aspects because if you're in business, your attitude to money is crucial to your success and is a good starting place.

Come and join me on the first steps of what I have found to be a fascinating, enjoyable, and richly rewarding journey!

1

Step One: Who's in Charge of Your Life?

When I was in my early twenties, after yet another break up with the latest boyfriend, I couldn't for the life of me work out why all my relationships kept 'going wrong'. Then I read a book called 'The Cinderella Complex', about relationships and how women behave in them. One point in particular made a huge impact on my life. I realised that all my past relationships had one thing in common – me! Even though I'd studied psychology and had some awareness about human behaviour, I hadn't clocked this. So I was compelled to see that *I* must therefore have had something to do with them all going 'wrong'. I tell you, this was a revelation that's affected my life ever since, because I was then able to see the possibility of affecting *why* these relationships had all turned sour. If it had something to do with me and my behaviour, well, I could change that. I might not be in charge of the relationship as a whole, but I certainly was in charge of how I behaved, and I could change if I wanted to. I started to think about how *I* was behaving in the relationship, instead of blaming the boyfriends.

So who's in charge of your life? You or another person?

You or your money? You or events in your world? If you're a Rich Thinker, you're someone who prefers to be in charge of your own life, rather than it being in charge of you. In the example above, I felt completely helpless and at a loss as to what to do. That was before I understood that I was the person in charge. That *what happens in my life was something to do with me!* Yes, it seems obvious, I know, but you'd be surprised how many people behave as if this isn't true even when they know this idea intellectually. Look at your own behaviour. Do you blame others when something goes 'wrong' in your life? Do you feel hard done by? Does life seem to be stacked against you and it's not fair? You can get stuck in the idea that these thoughts are facts, and they're not.

They are simply beliefs, that is, habitual thoughts, usually built up over a period of time. And any of these kinds of thoughts or beliefs are the complete opposite of rich thinking.

This willingness to stop blaming and start taking action in your own life to change things you're not happy with is at the core of rich thinking. Without it, you can be stuck in the deep, dark hole of blame, wallowing around, feeling awful, hopeless and helpless. The first step out is to see that it's *you* in the hole, and that only *you* can do something about it in order to get out.

Another example – many years ago, I went out with someone for a few months who I discovered later was a millionaire. I was really horrified when I realised that just because he had loads of money, (and I felt I had very little in comparison), I thought he ought to give me some! I was embarrassed to admit this to myself (and I certainly didn't admit it to anyone else, let alone him). However, if you're in a state in your life where you feel as if there's 'them' (the rich ones) and 'us' (the poor, or average earners) then I bet there are quite a few reading this who've had the same reaction to other people whom you perceive have lots of money.

It's so completely mad, this idea, it's almost funny! After all, why should someone give you money for no reason at all? I know people do, and that's great, but to *expect* it, just because they have money and you don't, is a sign of poor thinking. It's not the attitude of someone in charge of their lives. Rather it is the thinking of someone at the effect of others, ie taking on a victim role. It is 100% definitely NOT Rich Thinking. What *would* have been RichThinking was if I had been fired up myself by his story enough to want to do something different in my own life. He'd observed in his twenties that money could buy him the kind of freedom he wanted, and resolved there and then to become a millionaire by the time he was thirty, which he did. I could have done the same thing, but I wasn't ready for it; in fact, at that time it didn't even occur to me that I could make that decision too.

If you're not experiencing being in charge of your life, then it is very likely you will be blaming someone or something else for making sure you can't live your dreams/have what you want/be happy. You know you're blaming when you catch yourself thinking or saying:

- If only...
- It's not fair
- Why couldn't they have ...

Or maybe you don't notice the thoughts, but register the feelings associated with blame, a few of which may be resentment, irritation, feeling hard done by, indignation and so on. Ask yourself 'where am I trapped in the cold alleyway of blame?'

Be really honest with yourself – who are you blaming for your life or business not being the way you want it to be?

Step 1 Activity:

Start looking for the lesson underneath blame from which you can grow, and therefore free yourself.
  Use this statement to help turn round and see the only way out from the dead end alleyway blame:

What could I be doing for myself that I am currently not doing, because I am so busy blaming another?

Then take that action. For example, instead of blaming the economy as the reason you don't have enough money to do _____, choose to ask yourself a question beginning with *"How could I possibly..."*

Instead of blaming customers for not buying as much as you want them to buy, ask '*How could I possibly serve them better so that making a purchase seems like an obvious next step for them?"*

Instead of blaming your partner for causing you extra work, ask '*How could I possibly think about this differently?"*

Any sentence that begins with '*How could I possibly...*' opens a door to stepping out of being a victim of circumstances, no matter what they are.

2

Step Two: Listen to What You're Saying

Many people go around in their lives muttering. Often it's along the lines of, 'It isn't fair' or, 'It's all right for them, they've got plenty of money' or, 'I never seem to have enough time', or even, 'No matter how much I have of anything I have, it's never enough'. Muttering like this is connected with bitterness, complaining and, if it's about other people, gossip. Sometimes it's subconscious mutterings; unspoken, but even more powerful for that, because you don't necessarily realize you're doing it. Thinking like this, saying statements like these, is poor thinking, and you're really shooting yourself in the foot if you want to bring more success into your life and business. So, after Step One, taking charge, the second hugely important thing in thinking more richly is to become more conscious of what you're thinking, speaking and feeling.

Begin to listen - and even if you think you are someone who is very aware of what you say, keep an open mind and notice what you are *really* saying. For instance, notice how you react when:

- bills come into your business and/or personal life
- a colleague you know has many more clients than you
- you see something you want, but you think you can't afford to have

it
- you see others living a 'better' lifestyle than you
- you hate 'the new kid on the block' as they seem to be flavour of the month and you've been forgotten

If you're not sure, check out your feelings – they will definitely tell you what is going on.

Some years ago I caught myself feeling envious of someone who lived in a house I would have liked to live in. I felt cross, and irritable, and suddenly could only see everything that was 'wrong' in my life. I realised I must have been thinking poor thoughts, such as 'I wish I lived in that house', and 'It's not fair!' As soon as I noticed what I was doing, the alarm bells went off, and I veered away in my mind from that self-destructive path and deliberately began to focus on what I *did* have that I really appreciated. Result - I began to feel abundant once more; my heart opened again, and I felt more loving and generous to the world. Needless to say, I was much nicer to be around too.

So, would you rather feel happy or sad? Rich or poor? I assume as you're reading this, that you'd rather by happy and rich (or at least richer). So go back to the questions on the previous page and look again – check your reactions.

What do they tell you?

This is where being in charge of your life comes in – you know your thoughts are defining you, and you know that only you can do something about it. So with the thoughts you've just noticed or written down, try turning them into their opposites. Then see how you feel about them, just as I did with my house envy. If opposite seems too much, then focus on a thought that moves you in the direction of where you want to go.

For example:

Original thought and feeling:
Thought: *I hate those people who live in that house.*
Feeling: *envy.*

Midway thought and feeling:
Thought: *At least I've got a house I like to live in.*
Feeling: *lighter, more open.*

Ideal thought and feeling:
Thought: *What a beautiful house! I get such pleasure from looking at it.*
 Feeling: *appreciation.*

I can guarantee the feelings will be of a different nature than how you felt with the first, more limiting, thoughts.

Step 2 Activity:

Train yourself to listen better to the words you say out loud, and those that go on only inside your head. Choose to make these positive more often than not, and watch how your energy and feelings become more expansive and pleasant. Make this a self-care practice - associate it with something positive you do regularly, eg walking, meditating, swimming or other exercise. Or even just the ubiquitous teeth brushing!

Begin to listen - and even if you think you are someone who is very aware of what you say, keep an open mind and notice what you are *really* saying. For instance, notice how you react when:

3

Step Three: Welcome New Thoughts

None of this stuff works unless you put it into practice. So right now ask yourself do you want to be a Rich Thinker or a poor thinker? If you want to be the first, then begin to practice the kinds of thoughts rich thinkers think, and start to change your poor beliefs into rich ones. Start to realize the thoughts you'd rather not have are actually a great gift to you in that they can point you in the direction you **do** want to go.

So start by practicing some new thoughts now. Here are some examples (watch out for your mind which is likely to pooh-pooh this as if you believe the left hand thought, then you will definitely NOT believe the right hand one!

Poor Thinkers say:

1. I can't afford it
2. How can I afford it?
3. I'm always struggling
4. I welcome in ease and flow
5. I feel guilty when I spend money on myself
6. There are more important things in life than money

Rich Thinkers say:

1. I treat myself really well because I'm worth it and it's fun
2. Nothing works out for me
3. Things often work out well for me
4. I wish I had ____in my life/business
5. I'm willing to do what it takes to have ____in my life/business
6. I can have money and all the other things important to me too

Use these Rich Thoughts as replacements every time you notice your poor thoughts. Because you're trying to change a belief, you need to practice it regularly.

For instance, if you catch yourself thinking 'I'll never have enough money', you can change it to 'I always have enough money'. You need to practice this statement often to cut a new path through the jungle of beliefs you have to do with never having enough money. This may sound simple – after all 'it's only a thought, and a thought can be changed' (Louise L. Hay), but it's not necessarily easy.

Change the thought first, and what then happens is that your mind may rebel. After all, it's been thinking these poor thoughts all your life, why should it change now? We are fundamentally habitual in our behaviour, both in mind and body, and changing these habits requires us to make a decision to change, and follow through.

For example, a client of mine, Maggie, had recently realised that she was limiting herself when she thought 'I can't afford it'. It took her a while to understand this, because her financial situation was such that at the end of every month, she was always short of money. So she was proving to me, and herself, that she couldn't afford what she wanted (in this case a new dress to attend a wedding). I challenged her on this by asking her to start saying 'I can afford it'. This was very difficult for her because she just wanted to show me her bank statement to prove that she couldn't.

But I wasn't interested so much in her bank balance, as in her mind. After the second session, when she'd practiced changing the thought several times, and started work on attracting more clients, she spoke of something changing. Just by allowing herself to entertain the idea that she might be able to afford it, she then began to think about *how* she could manage to get that dress. And this is the process at work – she opened a door to the room in her mind that contained only limited thoughts. Opening the door meant that new thoughts could find their way in, paving the way for new beliefs. She was willing to think differently. The end result of this particular story was that out of the blue, her sister rang and said she wanted to buy her a new dress as a thank you for some childcare Maggie had done the previous month. Sounds a bit like magic, this bit, doesn't it? But I've seen things like this happen so many times that, not only do I no longer question it, I sit back and enjoy it.

So if you try changing your limiting thoughts and find it challenging, that's because it is. Everybody has an ingrained habitual way of thinking, and initially changing that to something else requires practice and persistence. That's why it's so much easier when you have support. For example, I always brush my teeth in the same way. I do it like this because I don't think about it – my hand has learnt where to go and I just do it. But if I try to change the method, boy, do I get unstuck! It's as if I've asked myself to do something really mind-blowingly difficult. But persistence with that means it becomes easier and easier, until finally the new tooth brushing routine becomes the norm. The same will happen with your new rich thoughts if you practice them. See my article *'Step by Step Rich Thoughts'* at https://www.janeduncanrogers.com

The other important thing about changing thoughts is getting into the feelings associated with them. Maggie in the above example walked down her local high street really imagining in the moment what it was like to be carrying the new dress she had in a bag. At that stage, she didn't really believe all this, she was just doing it for a bit of fun and because in the coaching session she'd agreed to do it. But it worked. She found she really enjoyed 'playing' in this way, with the result that as she walked down the street, she was benefiting from feeling rich and abundant already, even without the actual dress in reality. So really get into how it feels that life is flowing easily. For example, really let yourself imagine and/or remember what life is like when it is flowing easily – get into that space in your mind, regardless of outer circumstances. It doesn't matter if you don't experience that in actuality at this moment, because you're in the middle of changing your thoughts and behaviour. But incorporate the imagined feelings along with the new thoughts and have much more fun - it's incredibly effective, makes you feel good, and before you know it, you'll find that you're beginning to experience your life as flowing more smoothly.

Step 3 Activity:

Identify 3 limiting thoughts and feelings you have about your business and begin to change them using the Step by Step Rich Thoughts process, found at my website, www.janeduncanrogers.com

4

Step Four: Take Rich Actions

How can you be taking truly rich actions if you are having poor thoughts and feelings? You can't, because if your thoughts and feelings are poor ones, then by default actions resulting from these will be poor too. For example, Joyce was overheard to say 'Oh I really can't afford this expensive training, it's a huge amount of money'. She bought the training anyway, but was so overcome with feelings of guilt that she tried to get her place refunded. This kind of thing does happen, and maybe it's you that does it. The action of her buying the training was a poor one, because of the thinking and feeling behind it. The very same action could easily have been a rich one, where she decided in advance she was going make an investment in herself by purchasing the training she really wanted, regardless of the cost, finding a way to pay for it that would feel good and allow her to freely enjoy what she was learning. Then this very same action is a rich one.

So you have to be careful with apparently rich actions – they can look rich on the outside, but when you unpack what's behind them, they can, in fact, be very poor indeed.

Where it's really easy to see rich or poor actions taking place is in the buying of clothes. At least in the Western world, many clothes are so cheap these days that often people just buy them without thinking. My way of buying them now is to buy only those *items that make me feel rich when I put them on.* Quite simple really, and it's not necessarily to do with how much they cost. I don't buy from the cheap chain stores because the experience of buying these clothes doesn't make me feel rich. Instead, I look for quality items, wherever I can find them, that I feel really good in. Even if you have a limited clothing allowance, you can still discriminate between clothes that make you feel rich when you put them on, and those that don't.

Next time you're shopping, just ask yourself that crucial question – "Do I feel rich in this?" If the answer is no, consider why you would continue buying it, if your intention is to be a Rich Thinker.

Watch out for poor thinking, ie thinking that keeps you stuck – you appear as if you're rich, but your action is actually that of someone who is poor! This scenario is happening in millions of homes up and down the country. For example, people think that 'having what I want when I want it' is the action of a rich person. But funnily enough, truly rich thinkers are more likely to consider carefully when buying a big item, because they often like to invest their money in things that will produce an income for them later on. They decide they don't need to have the latest phone, the new style sofa, or the latest model of car, because they want to allocate that money to what they perceive is a better opportunity. Of course, there's likely to come a time in your life as a Rich Thinker where your disposable income for items such as a phone is more than enough, so you won't be thinking much about it at all, perhaps. Or maybe you'll be a Rich Thinker who wants to put all your excess monies into your favourite charity or foundation, or start a business. The point is, you will have choices. This step invites you to look very carefully at what you consider to be rich actions and what are not. Your neighbour up the street who's just bought a brand new BMW may appear to be rich, but it's quite possible they are struggling financially just as much as some other people.

Poor thinking says that what people have defines how rich they are.

Rich thinking says it's who people are, and how they behave that defines them.

If you're bringing in a huge income, but also have huge expenses, and worry about whether you can really pay for all the things you want, are you really any richer than the person who has a smaller income, smaller expenses, and lives a more modest lifestyle? I don't think so. However, where this becomes challenging is that old cliché 'keeping up with the Joneses'. People become enormously pressured by feeling that they have to join in with what their peer group is doing. It's much more difficult to drive an old banger of a car if the people you mix with enjoy new cars often. It makes you feel you have to do the same, even if your values are different, or you want to move from being a poor thinker to a Rich Thinker. So take note of peer pressure – it will be there, and to avoid being hooked back into that way of thinking, you have to be aware of what is happening. Feeling compelled to keep up with your friends is poor thinking, because it's not a choice. If you are consciously choosing to spend money you don't have because all your friends have the latest model of car, then that's also poor thinking. If you really want to move out into the world of 'rich thinking' then you're going to have to stand your ground when you decide to behave a bit differently in the future from what you have been doing. That may feel uncomfortable but you're changing, which is what you've said you want. And change by it's very nature brings discomfort, until you've got used to it, when it becomes familiar and you are at ease with it again.

Step 4 Activity:

Ask yourself every time you spend some money how you are feeling.

Stop spending in that moment if you are feeling anything less than great about what you are about to purchase. Ask yourself if the thing or experience you are about to buy will make you feel rich. If the answer is no, then wait to spend the money until you get a yes.

5

Step Five: Hang Out with Other Rich Thinkers

You're in charge of your life, you're listening to what you're thinking and saying, you're practicing rich thoughts as opposed to poor ones, and you're taking rich actions as a consequence. Step Five supports you in this process. Making rich thoughts more normal in your life is a lot easier if you hang out with other people who at the very least think positively about life, ie think richly.

Do you know someone who's an 'energy drain'? That is, someone whom you feel exhausted by after you've seen them, as if they've sucked all the energy out of you? Or perhaps you find yourself in conversation with them, being determinedly cheerful in the face of their pessimism and gloominess. That's exhausting too! Think of it like this – the amount of energy it takes you to resist being pulled into their bottomless pit could be much better spent thinking about strategies to make you more successful in your own life. And if you find you're colluding with them, and agreeing how awful life is, tut-tutting about this, that and the next thing, you're actually joining them; this is poor thinking, and not helpful. Do you really want to be doing this?

Poor thinkers tend to see other people's success as a threat – that's why they criticise, put down and judge. And this can be sometimes couched in terms called 'constructive criticism', or 'helpful feedback'. For instance, many years ago before the digital age, a friend of mine published an audiotape. While in theory I was all for this, keen on supporting her and wanting her to grow, in actuality I felt threatened by it, although I didn't fully realise it at the time. Surely I was the one who produced books and audiotapes, not her! She gave me a copy of it. I listened and the next time I met her, I focused on the one thing that I hadn't liked. (It was an excellent audio, and I was busy comparing myself with her and finding myself lacking). I told her how it could have been better when she next recorded, or produced some more. Even at the time I remember I didn't feel great about this, but I was too caught up in the poor thinking habits of comparison, judgement and fear to be able to extricate myself. Yes, we all do poor thinking from time to time, but make sure you aren't spending a lot of time with someone who is thinking poorly more often than not – and make sure you're not doing it either!

In fact, positive thinking people are more likely to have a rich experience of life simply because they tend to see the good things in a situation, rather than the bad. And this is a position in life where, quite simply, you have more fun. Of course, not everyone who's very positive has plenty of money – perhaps they have some money beliefs that have not yet been challenged, or are not very interested in money beyond having enough. But on the whole, you'll find that positive people are those who are happy with their lives, actively look to find the good in circumstances, and are generally pleasant to be around. So hang around them, not the nay-sayers, whom you really do not need to spend a lot of time with. Even if they are in your family! Seriously, think about it. How successful do you want your business or project to be? What are you willing to let go of to enhance your chances? Maybe you need to cut down how much you see that particular 'energy drain' and start being choosy around whom you spend your time.

One of the challenges with this is that people who tend to think negatively exert an enormous power in today's world. You only have to look at most of the media to see this, and because of this I don't bother reading the papers much anymore. If your circle of friends are people who tend to look on the gloomy side of life, you're going to have to step out on a limb if you want to think more positively. And this may not go down very well with them. So you have to be really clear about why you want to change your circumstances, and why this particular way, otherwise you'll feel doubtful. There's nothing a gloom and doom merchant likes better than someone who's trying to focus on the positive in life. They'll see you as a challenge to themselves to prove that everything really is awful and you're the poor soul who is full of delusions. Before you know it, you'll find yourself nodding in agreement with them when they pronounce on the state of the economy, why no-one can ever get what they want, etc etc. And then you wonder why you feel awful afterwards!

As well as spending time around positive people, spend time around others who are not only positive but are further ahead in business than you are in yours. Join a group of other people interested in these ideas. Then you'll be supporting each other on this journey, which is made considerably easier by support, by the way. Go to local events, take part in internet discussions, join online groups and forums, discover ways to discuss these ideas with others. Find the latest I am offering at https://www.janeduncanrogers.com

Step 5 Activity:

Do an inventory of the people in your life. List those you hang out with most often and get clear about whether they are supportive to be around or not. Actively choose to cut back the time you spend with those who can only see the negative side of life, and take up with others (face to face or online) who are supportive to you and your business.

6

Step Six: Understand How Luck Works

There are some things that can get in the way of rich thinking, and in my experience, thinking or feeling you are lucky can be one of them. You may never have been told it before, but being lucky can be bad news! Here's why:

People who look at someone else's success and enviously say 'she's so lucky' or 'some people get all the luck' are people who are making statements of lack, yes LACK, not luck. Statements of LACK keep you stuck. Focusing on someone else's 'luck' implies that you don't get to have any, as if there were presents being doled out by Father Christmas, except you missed out on your turn. And if you think you yourself are lucky, even though that may feel better, it's the other side of the same coin; it's still the same coin, and it's probably only a penny. It implies you're not in control, that it was all just an accident. How can you then repeat it if it's just luck?

Lucky or unlucky, either way no-one is taking responsibility here for anything that is going on in their lives at all. It's as if there's a Luck Fairy who capriciously waves her wand and blesses some and not others. Is life really like this? I don't think so.

Look at people you call 'lucky' and you'll see that they could often be described as making their own luck. My friend Peter is an example. He's known as the one who always lands on his feet. No matter what happens to him - and lots has – he's been like a cat, twisting himself in mid-air to fall safely on his feet again. For instance, he lost a job only to find a better one within a week. For many people, losing a job would have been a disaster. He saw it as an opportunity, taking the view that as it had happened, he'd better get on with life and make something out if it.

So what do you do if you want to change this thinking about luck?

Every time you hear yourself saying the word luck, or lucky, replace it with the word appreciate. Imagine it: you see someone whom you perceive 'has all the luck'. If the person is someone in the media, or someone you don't know personally, ask yourself, 'What do I appreciate about this person' or say,

"I appreciate what they are doing – I feel inspired by them."

If it's someone you know, say 'I really love that Anna is in my life', or 'I appreciate the experiences I have with Anna'. Then bring it back to yourself and practice appreciating what you DO have. When you envy something someone else has, you contract. Watch your energy the next time you feel envy. What happens in your body? It's almost as if your cells close up. At it's worst, it's corrosive and very close to bitterness. Not good for you and it tends to attract more of the same. Instead, choose expansion by noticing your envy, changing your thoughts and thereby your feelings.

You can create your own luck through your attitude. If your attitude is one where you focus on opportunities, you'll start to see them everywhere. Next time you find yourself wishing you were 'lucky', make a list (in your head is fine) of 50 things in your life you appreciate. I know, 50 sounds a lot, I used to think that too, but once you get going and really into it, you'll find it inspiring and want to keep on going. It feels fantastic to do, and changes your mood back to feeling good about your life. For instance, you might start by listing -

My computer
  My lovely office
  The sun shining today
  The buds on the trees opening outside my window
  My husband for being so good at fixing things
  My writing abilities
  My energy and enthusiasm
  My mentors
  The inventor of the telephone and internet

And so on (you can tell I'm at my desk at the moment!) Try it! It's one of the most powerful, and most simple things I know of to change how you are feeling. And when you change your feelings, through changing your thoughts, you're being a rich thinker and experiencing richness right now – all of which tends to attract riches of all kinds to you. Make it a daily practice of gratitude and expand your ability to feel good by doing so.

Step 6 Activity:
  Every time you catch yourself saying the word 'lucky' change it to grateful and notice how it makes you feel.

7

Step Seven: Take Charge of the Wishing Game

Another obstacle in the Rich Thinking journey is wishing. How many times have you been to supper with friends where the conversation turns to 'What I would do if I won the lottery'? It may provoke an interesting conversation. It looks like a fun game of imagining what you would do if the 'impossible' happened. But really what you're saying when you play the Wishing Game is things like 'I haven't got that much money', 'I don't really believe I'll ever have that much money', and 'It's safe to imagine this because I don't think it'll ever really happen'. Or something along those lines – that's if you think about it all. This is Wishing behaviour.

Wishing by its very definition keeps you in a place of stuckness. It's a bit like the dead-end alley of blame really, although it's a nicer place to hang out in. But it still keeps you stuck. People remain stuck because it's easier to stay in the relatively comfortable place of pretending. It's more challenging to make changes, especially if you think you don't like change very much. That's why it often takes a big life event, such as a loved one dying, becoming ill, redundancy, divorce etc before you are prised out of your safe shell to see what else life could bring you. This is why I never thought much about money before my late husband became ill with chronic fatigue, when we were suddenly compelled to re-look at it all, in the light of the possibility that he might never work again.

One of life's big challenges may or may not have happened to you; you might just have got fed up with the status quo and want to change. Either way, stop playing the Wishing Game and start playing a new game, one called The Rich Thinking Pledge. But before I tell you how to play, let me say something about commitment. Although many people baulk at that word, it's very likely to bring you exactly what you are committed to having in your life. Wow. Yes. Imagine it – if you are to get really serious about creating what you want in your life, make a 100% commitment. The commitment is to yourself. Not your partner, your business colleague, your children, your parents. Your Self.

This is a big deal if you are any kind of people pleaser, or were brought up with the belief 'If everyone else is happy, then I will be too'. Meaning you have to make sure others are happy first. With this kind of background, it can seem as if putting yourself first is selfish. But that's not the case. Putting yourself first is in fact a radical act of self-care, self-worth and self-love. And when you commit to yourself like this, your chances of what you want happening are hugely increased.

Now of course, this might mean you making some changes in your life. It might affect you in all sorts of ways, and you might not be willing to make those changes. In which case you'd have to accept where you are now, and be happy with that. And that's why most people don't even get near making a commitment in their lives – it's too uncomfortable. Nor do they want to admit this – so they just get on with playing the Wishing Game instead. No one realises they are in fact already committed to a poor thinking life, by default. Simply because they haven't applied Step One in their lives, they have chosen, inadvertently, to stick with limited thinking. Needless to say, I don't have much time for this. If you're really interested in becoming a Rich Thinker, and therefore becoming richer in all aspects of your life as well as your business, take a moment now to play a different game, the Rich Thinking Pledge.

Step 7 Activity:

When you catch yourself wishing for something, stop and ask yourself if you really want what you're wishing for or not. Be honest! If you do want it, choose to commit to doing what is necessary to have that thing or experience. Otherwise, drop it. It's keeping you limited.

8

Conclusion

Changing your mindset to one that invites more success into your life and business is one of the most challenging and rewarding things you can do. It is a full-on spiritual journey. Remember:

Rich thinking is an attitude, a commitment and a way of life.

That is what you are embarking on, or continuing with, when you practice these 7 steps.

If you want more support (and this journey is made a lot easier when you have support) then visit my website www.janeduncanrogers.com, and you'll find other resources to help you step more fully into being a Rich Thinker on a daily basis.

I really hope you have enjoyed reading this book as much as I have enjoyed writing it. Actually, I wrote the first edition in 2008 but never published it. It did need a few updates but not that many, as this mindset work is timeless.

If you found it helpful, I'd be delighted if you would leave a favourable review on Amazon!

About the Author

Having trained personally with Louise L Hay in 1990, Jane was the first person to bring her work to Europe and the UK, in the form of You Can Heal Your Life study groups.

Over the next ten years, she became well known in the personal development world, eventually publishing her first book, Choose Your Thoughts, Change Your Life in 1991. Having also trained as a counsellor and group leader, she developed a thriving therapy practice, while also owning and managing Oxfordshire's largest health clinic, the WellBeing Clinic.

Having sold this business, she and her husband lived in Ireland for a short while before moving to the north of Scotland, near to what was then the Findhorn Foundation Spiritual Community. At this point she trained as a coach, specialising in helping spiritual business owners achieve better results with ease, joy and grace.

Then her husband was diagnosed with cancer and died a year later. This changed everything, and led to another book, Gifted By Grief, her memoir of that time. Readers response to the chapter in there outlining the questions she had asked him before he died led to her founding her 6th small business, Before I Go Solutions®. This social enterprise trains lay and professional people to become End of Life Plan Facilitators, and help others get their end of life plans done before it's too late.

In 2023, Jane handed over the managing directorship of this business and took some time out. Recently she has returned to her first love, helping spiritual small business owners to develop their business with ease, joy and flow, by bringing in the practice of rich thinking.

Jane remarried in 2020 in between lockdowns, and in 2023 became Scotland's Woman of Inspiration, as awarded by the Association of Scottish Business Women. She loves to walk solo in the woods in the early morning, and her latest joy is riding a pony regularly, something she did a lot of as a child but has now taken up again.

You can connect with me on:
🌐 https://www.janeduncanrogers.com
f https://www.facebook.com/jane.duncanrogers

Subscribe to my newsletter:
✉ https://www.janeduncanrogers.com

Also by Jane Duncan Rogers

Current books available by Jane are below - all based on her experiences since her husband died in 2011 and which led to her founding the social enterprise, Before I Go Solutions®

Gifted By Grief: A True Story of Cancer, Loss and Rebirth
The story of how Jane and husband of 20 years, Philip, cope with the diagnosis in what turns out to be the final year of his life; what happens for Jane in the first year of debilitating grief, and how she gets through it into the beginning of a new kind of life.

She ends up stating something she would never have believed was possible:

I am grateful for both Philip's life AND his death.

Musings about the meaning of life and death, including excerpts from Philip's blog posts and Jane's journal entries at the time, are interwoven with funny, poignant and spiritually insightful stories.

Before I Go: The Essential Guide to Creating a Good End of Life Plan

A compassionate, practical guide to end-of-life matters, empowering you to clarify and share your wishes and continue to live life to the fullest.

Addresses the emotional, spiritual, and practical aspects of end-of-life planning to help you prepare well for your death

Enables the reader to make well-informed decisions about their end-of-life care and facilitate conversations with family and friends about this difficult topic

Includes guiding questions, exercises, and recording tools, as well as information sheets available for download and supportive online courses

Printed in Great Britain
by Amazon

40203573R00030